STEAM COOKING NOW!

By Barbara Swift Brauer

Illustrated by Dennis Redmond

OWLSWOOD PRODUCTIONS COOKBOOKS:

BUNDT CAKES by Karen Plageman and Susan Herbert
THE WOK WAY by Winnie Tuan
SLOW-CROCK COOKERY by Karen Plageman
THE CREPE BOOK by Susan Herbert
BRAVO! ITALIAN COOKING by Cynthia Scheer
BAKE BREAD by Marguerite Bencivenga and Barbara Brauer
FRENCH COUNTRY FAVORITES by Cynthia Scheer
NATURAL FIBER COOKING by Karen Plageman
GERMAN HOME COOKING by Cynthia Scheer
THE FOOD PROCESSOR BOOK by Pam Biele and Susan Walter
THE MICROWAVE WAY by Dorothy McNett
GOOD HEARTY SOUPS by Karen Plageman
MEXICAN COOKING by Cynthia Scheer
CHINESE COOKING by Mary W. Wilson
GREAT CASSEROLES! BY Karen Plageman
STEAM COOKING NOW! by Barbara Swift Brauer
CHICKEN FAVORITES by Mary Kay Hollander
GROUND BEEF FAVORITES by Barbara Swift Brauer

TABLE OF CONTENTS

INTRODUCTION

Join the steaming revolution now! Once relegated by western chefs to a few vegetables, steaming now takes its turn in America's kitchens. It's easy to see why. Working like an oven, a steamer fills quickly with moist, penetrating heat. The steam cooks foods gently, without destroying healthful nutrients, and moist heat brings out the delicious natural flavors of foods without drying. More efficient than oven baking, steaming saves you fuel dollars (you'll be amazed at the number of baked goods steaming makes even better).

Think a moment and you'll discover dozens of foods just meant for steaming. A steamer provides even, slow heat perfect for fresh vegetables, delicate seafood, egg dishes of all varieties and much, much more. Look over the recipe selection in STEAM COOKING NOW! and judge for yourself. Don't think because water is at the base of steam cooking that foods turn out soggy. Far from it! Casseroles, pasta dishes, desserts all cook to perfection. Use several steamer tiers and prepare a full dinner on one burner in no time at all. Try sea-fresh Steamed Clams in butter with corn on the cob and new potatoes. Enjoy a Mexican feast with Tortilla Wraps and Spanish Rice. Celebrate Sunday with Eggs Creole.

A few hints will assure you the best results:

—Cooking times given in the recipes are approximate. They are computed from the time the water in the steamer begins to boil (although you can place food in the steamer before). Check the food as necessary to judge cooking time.

—Make sure that you have a sufficient amount of water so that you can steam for the required period without worrying that the water will boil away. If steaming for long periods, check the water from time to time.

—Water must be boiling at all times. Bring water to a boil on high heat, then turn heat down to medium. The water should still be at an active boil. Some recipes specify "medium-low" or "medium-high" heat to indicate a necessary variation.

—To impart extra flavor to food you can add such seasonings as herbs, spices, onions, garlic and wine to steaming water. (See how this is done in Savory Chicken, page 27.)

—The recipes in STEAM COOKING NOW! are designed to fit the most popular-sized steamers. If you have a larger steamer you may double the recipes. Lengthen cooking time accordingly.

—If you are fortunate enough to have a multi-tiered steamer, whether bamboo or aluminum, you will enjoy steaming several dishes at once. Place those foods which require more cooking on the bottom layer where the heat is more intense and lighter foods, such as vegetables, on the upper tiers.

—Steam leftovers! You can reheat pasta, sandwiches, pizzas, anything. Place day-old bread directly on steamplate and steam it fresh in minutes.

—Steaming is an excellent substitute for blanching. Vegetables which need to be partially cooked or softened before being added to other recipes may be steamed for a few minutes. As a rough estimate, steam them half the time it takes to cook them, or just until they begin to soften.

EQUIPMENT

The equipment you'll need for steaming is readily available. Whether you choose to purchase a complete steamer, steaming accessories or assemble your own makeshift steamer from items you already have, you will have no trouble finding what you need.

The bamboo steamer comes from the Orient where it was designed to be used in a wok. (There is, however, a bamboo steamer available now with its own aluminum pot which holds more water allowing you to steam longer without worry and frees your wok for other cooking.) Available in various sizes from 4 to 12 inches, bamboo steamers are famous for their many stackable tiers which allow you to steam a whole meal on one burner. Another advantage is the woven bamboo lid that absorbs condensed water that otherwise might fall back into the food. The attractive, rapidly cooled basket doubles as a unique serving dish. Before using your bamboo steamer for the first time, scrub the bamboo thoroughly and, while it is still wet, steam it for 30 minutes. Store bamboo steamer in a well ventilated place to protect against mildew. If after use cleaning is necessary, scrub well in hot water with only a mild detergent.

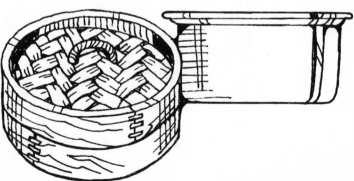

The aluminum steamer usually consists of two pots, a lid and an inner steamplate. Some sets also include several tiers so that you can efficiently steam more than one dish at a time. The upper tiers have a perforated bottom through which the steam rises. Foods may be placed directly on the steamplate or in heatproof dishes. Aluminum steamers are available in various diameters; they are easily cleaned, durable and efficient.

Other steamers, including an *enameled steel steamer* originating in Poland and an *Ironstone steamer*, which features a chimney in the center, may also be purchased at gourmet and housewares stores.

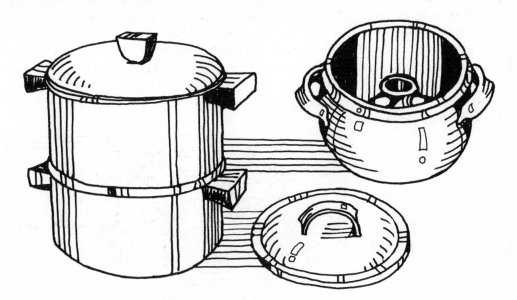

Accessories Among the many accessories you can purchase to transform a large pot or wok into a steamer with a minimum of effort and expense are:

Metal and wooden racks which support a heatproof dish over boiling water in a large pot or wok.

Bamboo and aluminium trays which fit against the sloping sides of a wok.

Colanders of every description which are perfect for steaming foods not requiring a dish.

Collapsible steel vegetable steamers for steaming vegetables and other foods not requiring a dish. Used with a covered saucepan, the overlapping petals adjust to fit large or small pans.

Artichoke steamers, designed to hold artichokes and cauliflower over boiling water. Their sturdy construction also makes them useful for supporting loaf pans or casseroles above boiling water.

Steaming dishes The problem with selecting heatproof dishes suitable for use in steamers is not finding one that will work, but deciding which to choose. There are so many! In gourmet shops and housewares stores, look over their selection of au gratin dishes, soufflé dishes and ramekins. All these special containers are heatproof and come in a variety of sets and sizes. At grocery and housewares stores you can find Pyrex dishes in various shapes and forms. And don't forget the disposable foil pans found at any grocery store.

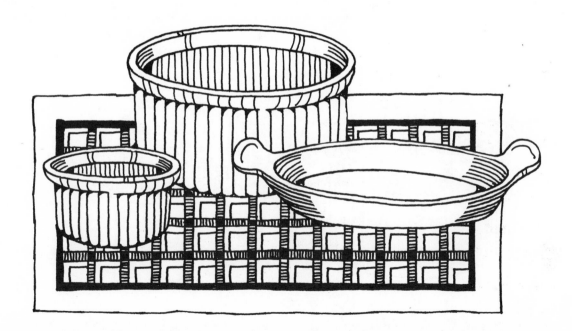

The recipes in STEAM COOKING NOW! are designed for the most common size steamers—8 to 10 inches. Many recipes specify a 7-inch pie pan or a 1 to 1-1/2 quart dish. Measure the diameter of your steamer or wok to see what size dishes it can accommodate. Next, be sure that the dishes you select are heatproof; be sure that they fit completely inside, allowing the steamer lid to rest snugly in place. When in the steamer, a dish must not cover all the perforations but allow the steam to circulate throughout the steamer.

You may find that some recipes call for containers (such as loaf pans) which may not fit inside your steamer. If so, you can improvise a steamer from a large pot or divide the recipe among several smaller containers, such as miniature loaf pans or muffin cups. Imagine individual servings of Brown Bread, Macaroni and Cheese or Spinach Rice! Remember that foods in small containers will cook faster so shorten cooking time accordingly.

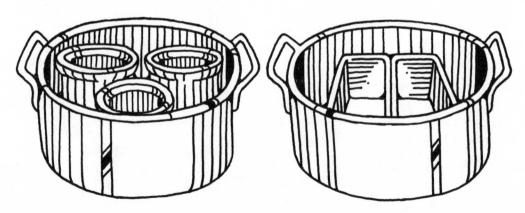

GARDEN FRESH VEGETABLES & DRESSINGS

Discover how delicious vegetables were meant to be! Unlike boiling, steaming cooks vegetables gently, allowing them to retain their natural nutrients, color and flavor. (Many vitamins, for example, dissolve in boiling water and so are thrown away.) And with steaming, you're less likely to overcook vegetables—remember that they should be *al dente,* or tender crisp.

Place vegetables directly on steamplate or in colander or heatproof dish that will fit inside steamer. Arrange them loosely so that steam can circulate freely. Make layers no deeper than 1-1/2 inches. If you have more vegetables than can fit into one steamer tray, add another tier.

Don't forget that steaming is superb for frozen vegetables, too. Steam 10 minutes, or until hot.   11

Acorn and Other Winter Squash: Cut squash open and remove seeds. Slice into serving portions. Place cut side down on steamplate or colander. Steam 30 to 45 minutes, or until tender when tested with a fork. Serve with butter or Brown Sugar Glaze (see recipe page 16).

Artichokes: Select artichokes with tightly closed leaves and good color, avoiding bruised ones. Before cooking, rinse and trim leaves and stem. Steam 30 to 45 minutes (depending on size) or until tender when pierced with a fork. Serve hot with melted butter or chilled with mayonnaise.

Asparagus: Choose well formed stalks with tightly closed buds. Before cooking, wash and snap off root ends. Steam whole stalks for 8 to 10 minutes; or slice stalks diagonally in 1 inch lengths and steam for 4 to 5 minutes. Serve with butter, Oriental Sauce (see recipe page 17) or Hollandaise Sauce (see recipe page 24).

Beets: Select small beets of uniform size. Before cooking, do not peel but trim and rinse. Steam whole beets for 30 to 45 minutes (depending on size) or until tender when pierced with a fork. Then, peel and slice. If necessary steam beets briefly to reheat before serving with butter. Or serve sliced, chilled beets in salads.

Bell Peppers: Whether buying red or green peppers, select firm, unblemished ones. Before cooking, rinse and core, then slice, chop or leave whole as desired. To steam whole, unstuffed peppers, place top side down and steam 5 to 8 minutes, or until tender crisp. Steam sliced or chopped peppers 5 to 8 minutes. Stuff whole peppers with filling, if desired, and steam 10 to 15 minutes. You may also combine chopped or sliced bell peppers with onions and serve with Oriental Sauce.

Broccoli: Buy bunches of broccoli with tightly closed buds, avoiding any which have a yellow tinge. Before cooking, wash thoroughly. To serve in stalks, cut each stem lengthwise so that it is 1/2 to 1 inch thick. Steam 8 to 15 minutes, or until tender crisp. Or, slice broccoli, cutting stem diagonally into 1/2 inch slices and flowerettes into bite-size pieces. Steam 5 to 8 minutes. Serve with butter, Cheese Sauce (see recipe page 16) or Oriental Sauce.

Brussels Sprouts: Select small, bright green heads with compact leaves. Before cooking, wash and trim. Steam 10 to 15 minutes, or until tender when pierced with a fork. Serve tossed with butter.

Cabbage: Whatever type you are buying, whether green, red or Chinese cabbage, buy fresh colored, unbruised heads. Before cooking, remove any discolored leaves and rinse. Cut into wedges and steam 10 to 15 minutes. Or, shred cabbage and steam 3 to 4 minutes. Serve with butter or Oriental Sauce.

Carrots: Avoid buying cracked, limp or rubbery carrots. For best flavor, buy baby carrots, rinse and steam whole for 10 minutes. Or, scrub and slice large carrots into 1/2 inch slices or matchsticks; steam these 8 to 10 minutes, or until tender when pierced with a fork. You can even shred carrots so that they require just 2 to 3 minutes of steaming. Serve with butter or Brown Sugar Glaze.

Cauliflower: Choose a white, unbruised head with fresh looking leaves. Before cooking, remove and discard leaves; rinse white flowerettes and cut them into bite-size pieces. Steam 5 to 7 minutes. Serve with butter or Cheese Sauce.

Corn on the Cob: Buy ears with firm, close set kernals and good color. Before steaming, remove husks and silk fibers, rinsing thoroughly in cold water. Break into smaller pieces to fit inside steamer, if necessary. Steam 10 to 15 minutes, or until tender when pierced with a fork. Serve with butter.

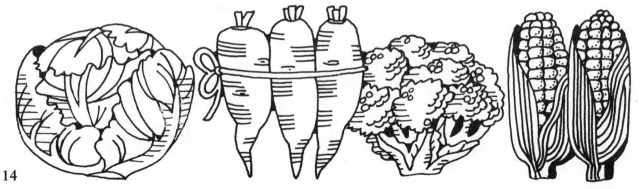

Green Beans: Purchase beans which are unbroken and have a good color. Before cooking, rinse and snap off stem ends. Steam whole beans 8 to 10 minutes; or slice beans diagonally into 1 inch lengths and steam 5 to 6 minutes. Serve tossed with butter or Oriental Sauce.

Pearl Onions: Select small onions of uniform size. Trim off root end and steam onions 10 minutes without peeling. Remove onions from steamer and slide peels off. Serve with Cheese Sauce.

Potatoes: Peel or scrub potato thoroughly. Cut into 1/2 inch slices and steam 10 to 12 minutes, or until tender when pierced with a fork. Steam whole new potatoes for 30 to 35 minutes, or until tender. Plan on steaming whole large potatoes 40 to 45 minutes or until tender. Serve white potatoes with butter or Creamy Dill Sauce (see recipe page 17); serve yams and sweet potatoes with butter or Brown Sugar Glaze.

Spinach and Other Greens: Buy fresh, crisp leaves with good color. Rinse thoroughly and trim root ends. Steam 2 to 3 minutes, or until limp. Drain thoroughly. Serve with butter or Oriental Sauce.

Zucchini and Other Summer Squash: Buy firm, unbruised squash. Before cooking, scrub well and cut into 1/2 inch slices. Steam 4 to 5 minutes, or until tender crisp when pierced with a fork. Do not overcook. Serve with butter or Oriental Sauce.

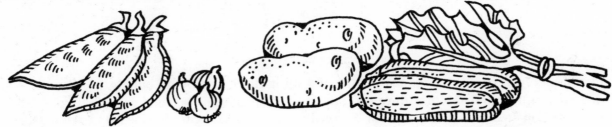

BROWN SUGAR GLAZE

2 tablespoons butter
1/8 teaspoon allspice
1/4 teaspoon salt
1/8 teaspoon pepper
2 teaspoons brown sugar

In a saucepan over low heat, melt butter and stir in allspice, salt and pepper. Add sugar and cook, stirring constantly, until bubbly and sugar is dissolved. Serve at once. Makes approximately 3 tablespoons. Recipe may be doubled.

CHEESE SAUCE

1 tablespoon butter or margarine
1 tablespoon all-purpose flour
1/2 cup milk
1/3 cup shredded cheddar cheese
dash cayenne
dash salt

In a small saucepan over low heat, melt butter and stir in flour. Cook until bubbly. Slowly add milk, stirring constantly, until mixture thickens. Stir in cheddar cheese, cayenne and salt, cooking only until cheese is melted and sauce is smooth. Serve at once. Makes 3/4 cup. Recipe may be doubled.

CREAMY DILL SAUCE

1/2 cup sour cream
2 teaspoons lemon juice
1 teaspoon dill weed
1/4 teaspoon salt
1/4 teaspoon pepper
1 green onion, finely minced
1/2 teaspoon sugar
1/4 cup buttermilk *or* 2 tablespoons whole milk

In a small bowl, combine sour cream, lemon juice, dill weed, salt, pepper, green onion and sugar. Blend in buttermilk. Cover and let rest for at least 2 hours. (Sauce may be made ahead and refrigerated up to 2 weeks in a tightly sealed container.) If serving over hot vegetables, serve at room temperature. If used as a salad dressing, chill thoroughly. Makes approximately 3/4 cup. Recipe may be doubled.

ORIENTAL SAUCE

1 tablespoon peanut oil
1 tablespoon oriental oyster sauce or soy sauce, at room temperature

Heat peanut oil until sizzling; drizzle oyster sauce and then hot oil over food. Serve at once. Makes 2 tablespoons. Recipe may be doubled.

STUFFED ZUCCHINI
a popular vegetable with flavorful stuffing

3 medium-size zucchini
3 tablespoons butter or margarine
3/4 cup dry bread crumbs
1/4 cup finely chopped fresh parsley
1/2 cup shredded cheddar cheese
2 pieces bacon, cooked until crisp and crumbled

Halve zucchini lengthwise and carefully scoop out seeds and pulp. Mince seeds and pulp and set aside. In a small saucepan, melt butter and stir in bread crumbs, zucchini seeds and pulp, parsley, cheese and crumbled bacon. Stuff zucchini shells with crumb mixture and place directly on steamplate or in a heatproof dish that will fit inside steamer. Steam 10 to 15 minutes, or until zucchini is just tender. Makes 6 servings.

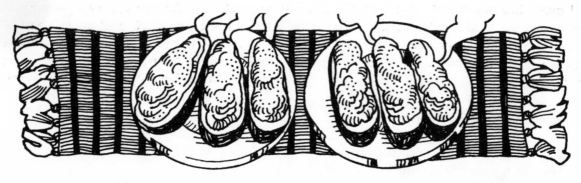

VEGETABLES PROVINÇAL
serve this in shallow bowls with French bread for a continental luncheon

1 clove garlic, finely minced
2 cups cubed eggplant
1/2 teaspoon oregano
1/2 teaspoon basil
1 small zucchini, cubed
1 small onion, sliced
1 medium-size ripe tomato, cut into 8 wedges
1 small green pepper, sliced
1/4 cup olive oil
1 beef or chicken bouillon cube
1/4 cup Parmesan cheese

In a 1 quart heatproof dish that will fit inside steamer place garlic and eggplant; sprinkle with oregano and basil. Add zucchini, onion, tomato and green pepper. Drizzle olive oil over all. Steam 15 to 20 minutes, or until vegetables are tender. Drain vegetables, reserving liquid. Remove vegetables to serving dish and keep warm. To reserved liquid in steaming dish add bouillon cube and stir until dissolved. Pour sauce over vegetables and top with Parmesan cheese. Serve at once. Makes 6 servings.

STUFFED TOMATOES
a colorful entrée for a light luncheon

6 large, ripe tomatoes
2 tablespoons butter or margarine
1/2 cup diced onion
1/2 cup diced green pepper
1/2 cup diced celery
2 cups shell macaroni, cooked according to package directions
3/4 cup shredded cheddar cheese
salt
pepper

Cut a thin slice off the top of each tomato. Carefully scoop out pulp and seeds; reserve these for other uses. Set tomato shells aside. In a small saucepan, melt butter and sauté onion, green pepper and celery for 3 to 5 minutes, or until onion is soft but not browned. Remove from heat and stir in macaroni and 1/2 cup cheese. Season with salt and pepper to taste. Stuff tomato shells with macaroni mixture. Sprinkle each tomato with remaining cheddar cheese. Steam 10 minutes, or until tomato is tender. Makes 6 servings.

LIGHT MEALS & SIDE DISHES

BUSY DAY MACARONI AND CHEESE
why bake? steam this ready in a jiffy

6 ounces shell macaroni,
  cooked according to package directions
2 cups shredded cheddar cheese
4 eggs, slightly beaten
2 green onions, minced

1/2 teaspoon Worcestershire sauce
1/4 teaspoon Tabasco sauce
1/2 teaspoon celery salt
1/4 teaspoon pepper

In a large bowl, combine macaroni, 1-1/2 cups cheese, eggs, onions, Worcestershire sauce, Tabasco sauce, celery salt and pepper. Stir to combine. Pour into a lightly greased 1-1/2 quart heatproof dish that will fit inside steamer. Steam 20 to 30 minutes, or until center is firm. Makes 4 servings.

SPANISH RICE
a meatless version of this classic with fluffy rice and tender vegetables

1-1/2 cups uncooked long grain rice
1 (8 oz.) can tomato sauce
1/4 cup red wine or chicken broth
1 cup water
1 cup minced onion
1 cup minced celery
1 cup chopped artichokes (optional)
1 clove garlic, minced
1 tablespoon olive oil
1 large bay leaf
1/2 teaspoon basil
1 teaspoon salt
fresh parsley sprigs, for garnish

In a greased 1-1/2 quart heatproof dish that will fit inside steamer, combine uncooked rice, tomato sauce, wine, water, onion, celery, artichokes, garlic, oil, bay leaf, basil and salt. Stir to mix thoroughly. Steam 40 to 50 minutes, stirring occasionally, or until rice is tender and liquid is absorbed. Garnish with fresh parsley sprigs. Makes 6 servings.

RICE AND SPINACH MOLD
you'll enjoy this nutritious dish as an entrée and a side dish

2 cups cooked rice, white or brown
2 eggs
1 cup cottage cheese
1 cup shredded cheddar cheese
1/4 cup chopped fresh parsley
2 cups finely chopped fresh spinach, firmly packed
1/2 teaspoon paprika
1/2 teaspoon salt
1/4 teaspoon pepper
2 green onions, finely minced
1/2 cup plain yogurt

In a large bowl, combine rice, eggs, cottage cheese, cheddar cheese, parsley, spinach, paprika, salt, pepper and green onions. Spoon into a well greased 7-inch ring mold* and steam 15 to 20 minutes or until set. Unmold onto serving plate and dollop with yogurt. Makes 4 servings.

*Note: if you do not have a 7-inch ring mold, place a muffin tin or custard cup in the center of a deep 7-inch pan and spoon rice mixture around cup.

POACHED EGGS IN HOLLANDAISE SAUCE
eggs steam perfectly every time

8 eggs
Hollandaise Sauce (recipe follows)
fresh parsley or paprika, for garnish
4 English muffins, split and toasted

Lightly butter individual heatproof dishes. Gently break 2 eggs into each. Steam 5 to 10 minutes, or until egg whites are firm. While eggs are steaming, prepare Hollandaise Sauce. Spoon over eggs, garnish with parsley or paprika and serve at once with English muffins. Makes 4 servings.

HOLLANDAISE SAUCE

2 egg yolks
1 tablespoon lemon juice
1/4 teaspoon salt
1/8 teaspoon paprika
1/3 cup butter

In a blender or food processor, blend egg yolks, lemon juice, salt and paprika. In a saucepan, melt butter and allow to cool slightly. With blender or food processor on, slowly pour in butter in a thin stream. Blend until smooth and serve at once.

HUEVOS RANCHEROS
the festive flavors of Mexico make a brunch-time favorite

2 tablespoons lard or vegetable shortening
1 small onion, chopped
1 clove garlic, minced
1/2 teaspoon cumin
1 teaspoon oregano
1 (4 oz.) can diced green chiles
1 large tomato, seeded and coarsely chopped
1 small avocado, sliced
8 eggs
1/2 cup shredded cheddar or Monterey jack cheese
1 (9 oz.) package tortilla chips

In a large saucepan, heat lard and sauté onion, garlic, cumin and oregano until onion is soft but not browned. Remove from heat and add chiles and tomato. Divide mixture evenly among 4 individual heatproof dishes. Top with avocado slices. Gently break 2 eggs onto each serving and garnish with shredded cheese. Steam 10 to 15 minutes, or until egg whites are firm. Serve at once with tortilla chips. Makes 4 servings.

EGGS CREOLE
make the tomato sauce the night before for easy morning assembly

2 pieces bacon *or* 2 tablespoons oil
1/2 cup chopped onion
1/2 cup chopped green pepper
1/8 teaspoon Tabasco sauce
1 cup thinly sliced okra, fresh, frozen or canned
1 (15 oz.) can tomatoes, chopped, and their liquid
1/2 teaspoon salt
1/4 teaspoon pepper
1 cup cooked rice
8 eggs
toast points for garnish

In a saucepan, fry bacon until crisp. Remove bacon and drain on paper towel. In bacon drippings (or oil), sauté onion and green pepper until onion is soft but not browned. Drain off any excess fat. Add Tabasco, okra and tomatoes. Simmer, uncovered, 10 minutes, or until okra is soft. Stir in salt, pepper and rice. Distribute mixture evenly among 4 individual heatproof dishes. Gently break 2 eggs onto each and sprinkle with crumbled bacon. Steam 10 minutes or until egg whites are firm. Garnish each serving with toast points and serve at once. Makes 4 servings.

ENTRÉES MEANT FOR STEAMING

SAVORY STEAMED CHICKEN
the wine mixture used for steaming becomes an exquisite sauce

1 chicken (about 2 to 3 lbs.), quartered
pepper
paprika
2 cups white wine
2 cups water
1/2 teaspoon tarragon
1 teaspoon thyme

1 bay leaf
1/4 teaspoon rosemary
1 small onion, quartered
2 tablespoons all-purpose flour
1 teaspoon sugar
1/2 cup cold water
2 beef or chicken bouillon cubes

Skin chicken if desired. Sprinkle pieces with pepper and paprika to taste. Place chicken on steamplate or in heatproof dish that will fit inside steamer. In steam pot, combine wine, water, tarragon, thyme, bay leaf, rosemary and onion. Bring this mixture to boil and place chicken over it to steam 35 to 40 minutes, or until chicken is tender. In a saucepan, blend flour and sugar in cold water. When chicken is done, remove from steamer and keep warm. Bring steaming liquid to a rapid boil, add bouillon cubes and continue to boil for 5 minutes. Strain liquid and add to saucepan. Bring to a boil, stirring constantly, and cook until thickened. Serve sauce with chicken. Makes 4 servings.

VERY SPECIAL MEAT LOAF
cheese is the secret ingredient in this family favorite

3/4 pound extra lean ground beef
1/4 cup rolled oats
1/4 cup milk
1 egg
1 teaspoon salt
1/2 teaspoon pepper
1 stalk celery, finely chopped
1/2 cup finely chopped onion
1-1/2 cups shredded cheddar cheese
1/4 cup catsup

In a large bowl, combine beef, oats, milk, egg, salt, pepper, celery, onion and 1 cup cheddar cheese, using your hands to blend thoroughly. Place meat mixture in a 7-inch pie pan, molding into an even, rounded shape. Top with catsup and remaining 1/2 cup cheddar cheese. Steam 25 to 30 minutes, or until pink is gone from center. Makes 4 servings.

TORTILLA WRAP-UPS
serve piping hot with Spanish Rice and a green salad

1/4 pound ground beef
1 small onion, chopped
1 (6 oz.) can tomato paste
1/4 cup red wine or water
1 cup refried beans, homemade or canned
1/2 teaspoon cumin

1/2 teaspoon chile powder
1/2 pound Monterey jack cheese
8 corn tortillas
1/2 cup sour cream
1 (2.3 oz.) can sliced black olives
1 green onion, minced

In a skillet, brown beef and onion until beef is crumbly and onion is soft. Drain off any excess fat and stir in tomato paste, wine, beans, cumin and chile powder. Blend thoroughly and simmer, uncovered, 5 to 10 minutes, adding more water if necessary. Cut jack cheese into sticks 1/2 by 1/4 by 2 inches. Set aside. Soften tortillas as needed by placing in an uncovered steamer 1 to 2 minutes or until pliable. On each tortilla, spread 2 tablespoons meat filling down the center and top with a stick of jack cheese. Fold tortilla edges over to conceal filling, fold in ends and place seam side down in a heatproof dish that will fit inside steamer. Steam 15 minutes, or until heated through. Garnish each serving with sour cream, black olives and green onions. Makes 4 servings.

29

SPAGHETTI AND HAM CASSEROLE
children love the rich tomato flavor

1/2 pound spaghetti, cooked according to package directions
1 (6 oz.) can tomato paste
1 (15 oz.) can tomatoes, chopped, and their liquid
1 cup cubed ham
1/2 teaspoon basil
1/2 teaspoon chile powder
1/4 teaspoon dry mustard
1/2 teaspoon salt
1/2 cup Parmesan cheese

In a large bowl, combine cooked spaghetti and tomato paste, and stir to mix well. Stir in tomatoes, their liquid, ham, basil, chile powder, mustard and salt. Mix thoroughly and place in a greased 1-1/2 quart heatproof dish that will fit inside steamer. Top with Parmesan cheese and steam 20 minutes, or until heated through. Makes 6 servings.

TURKISH STUFFED GREEN PEPPERS
peppers with curried filling steamed to perfection!

1 pound ground lean lamb
1/2 teaspoon curry powder
1 onion, chopped
1 cup raisins
1/2 cup slivered almonds
2 cups cooked rice
4 to 6 large green peppers

In a large skillet, cook lamb, curry powder and onion until lamb is browned and crumbly and onion is soft. Drain off excess fat and stir in raisins, almonds and rice. Mix thoroughly and set aside. Carefully cut around the stem of each green pepper and remove core and seeds. Stuff each pepper with rice mixture. Place directly on steamplate or in a heatproof dish that will fit inside steamer. Steam 10 to 15 minutes, or until peppers are tender crisp. Makes 4 to 6 servings.

Note: If pepper is too tall to fit upright in steamer, cut each pepper in half lengthwise and then stuff with filling.

31

ZUCCHINI MANICOTTI
a vegetarian dish you'll share with family and friends

2 tablespoons vegetable oil
1 small onion, chopped
1 clove garlic, minced
1 (8 oz.) can tomato sauce
1/2 cup water
1/2 teaspoon oregano
1/2 teaspoon basil
1 tablespoon chopped fresh parsley
8 ounces mozzarella cheese, shredded

1 cup shredded zucchini
2 eggs
1/4 teaspoon allspice
1/2 teaspoon salt
1/8 teaspoon pepper
1 (3.75 oz.) package manicotti shells (8 shells in all) cooked according to package directions
1/4 cup Parmesan cheese

In a skillet, heat oil and sauté onion and garlic until onion is soft but not browned. Stir in tomato sauce, water, oregano, basil and parsley. Simmer uncovered 5 to 10 minutes. In a small bowl, combine mozzarella, zucchini, eggs, allspice, salt and pepper. With a small spoon, stuff manicotti shells with zucchini mixture. Arrange filled manicotti shells in a single layer in a shallow heatproof serving dish that will fit inside steamer. Cover with sauce and sprinkle with Parmesan cheese. Steam 15 to 20 minutes, or until heated through. Makes 4 servings.

HAM AND MUSHROOM QUICHE
a unique quiche with a crust of brown rice

1-1/2 cups cooked brown rice
1 teaspoon prepared mustard
3 eggs
1/4 teaspoon brown sugar
1/2 teaspoon salt
1/4 teaspoon pepper
1/2 cup shredded Swiss cheese
1 cup diced ham
1/2 cup thinly sliced fresh mushrooms *or* 1 (4 oz.) can sliced mushrooms, drained
1 green onion, sliced

In a medium-size bowl, combine rice, mustard, 1 egg and brown sugar. Spread mixture evenly in the bottom and up the sides of a greased 7-inch pie pan. In another bowl, beat 2 eggs with salt and pepper until light in color. Stir in Swiss cheese, ham and mushrooms. Pour into pie pan. Steam 20 to 25 minutes, or until center is set. Garnish with green onions. Makes 4 servings.

SELECT FROM THE SEA

You'll find that steaming brings out the delicate flavor of fresh seafood better than any other type of cooking. For best results, use seafood as soon as possible after purchase. If frozen, thaw seafood in the refrigerator (not at room temperature) and use within 24 hours. Do not refreeze.

Clams: For steaming whole clams, select only the hard shell or soft shell varieties. (Other types, such as Razor, Pismo and Geoduck clams must be cleaned and their entrails removed before eating.) Buy clams alive in the shell, avoiding those which are cracked or broken, or which do not close when touched. Place clams in salted water to cover and sprinkle 1/4 cup cornmeal over clams. Allow to stand several hours. Drain and rinse. Before steaming, scrub clams under cold running water with a stiff bristled brush to remove all dirt. Place clams in steamer, either directly on steamplate or on a heatproof dish that will fit inside steamer. Steam 5 to 10 minutes, depending on the number of clams, until the shells open. Discard any clams which are still closed. Serve at once with drawn (clarified) butter. Or, remove clams from shells and chill in the refrigerator to serve with Cocktail Sauce (see recipe page 40).

Mussels: Scrape barnacles off outside of shell, scrub mussels under cold running water with a stiff bristled brush and follow procedure for steaming clams.

Oysters: Scrub oysters thoroughly under cold running water with a stiff bristled brush and follow procedure for steaming clams.

Shrimp or prawns: Shrimp may be shelled and deveined either before steaming or after, as you prefer. To clean shrimp, peel off shell and remove legs and tail. With a knife or toothpick, remove the dark blue vein just under the skin down the back. Place shrimp either directly on steamplate or in a heatproof dish that will fit inside the steamer. Steam 5 to 8 minutes or until they are pink and firm.

Cooked shellfish: Many types of shellfish come from the market already cooked. To reheat cooked shellfish, such as crab or frozen and thawed lobster, steaming is preferable to boiling. Transfer seafood from any chilled container directly to either steamplate or a heatproof dish that will fit inside steamer. Arrange food loosely so that steam will circulate evenly. Steam only a few minutes and check to see if food is heated through. Remember, steaming warms foods rapidly.

Fish: When buying unfrozen fish in whatever form, whether fillet, steak or whole, make sure it is fresh. The fish should have a light, pleasant odor and be firm to the touch. If buying frozen fish, make sure it is still solidly frozen, that there is no odor or discoloration.

To steam, place fish in a heatproof serving dish that will fit inside steamer or place fish directly in a cradle of cheesecloth or linen to allow for easy removal. The amount of time required for steaming fish is very short: approximately 10 minutes per pound. Fish is done when it flakes easily when tested with a fork.

SIMPLE STEAMED FISH
this basting sauce brings out the succulence of fresh fish

1/4 cup butter
1 tablespoon chopped chives
1-1/2 teaspoons lemon juice
2 tablespoons white wine
2 pounds fish fillets or steaks

In a saucepan, melt butter and stir in chives, lemon juice and wine. Heat briefly to blend. Place fish in a heatproof dish that will fit inside steamer and spoon sauce over fish. Steam 8 to 10 minutes or until fish flakes easily when tested with a fork. Makes 4 servings.

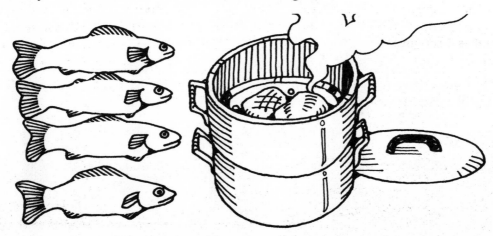

MUSHROOM FISH FILLETS
serve with a fresh green salad and steamed potatoes for a simple, perfect meal

1-1/2 pounds fish fillet
6 tablespoons butter
2 tablespoons white wine
1/2 teaspoon tarragon
1/4 pound fresh mushrooms, sliced *or* 2 (4 oz.) cans button mushrooms
1/4 cup chopped fresh parsley

Bring fish to room temperature and set aside. In a 1 quart heatproof dish that will fit inside steamer, dot bottom with 2 tablespoons butter; arrange fish fillets in an even layer. In a skillet, melt remaining butter and stir in wine and tarragon. Sauté mushrooms in wine mixture until soft and arrange over fish. Garnish with chopped parsley and steam 10 to 15 minutes, or until fish flakes easily when tested with a fork. Makes 4 servings.

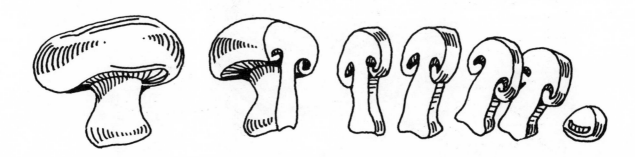

CHINESE STYLE STEAMED FISH
learn the simple secret of preparing whole fish deliciously

1 whole fish (trout, flounder or sea bass), about 1-1/2 pounds, cleaned and scaled
4 slices fresh ginger root
3 green onions, 2 whole and 1 minced
2 teaspoons sherry
1 tablespoon soy sauce
1-1/2 tablespoons peanut oil

Place fish on a heatproof dish that will fit inside steamer. Arrange ginger and 2 whole green onions on top of fish. Steam fish 10 to 15 minutes, or until it flakes easily when tested with a fork. Meanwhile, combine sherry and soy sauce. Set aside. In a small saucepan, heat peanut oil until sizzling. When fish is done, remove green onions and ginger and drizzle soy sauce mixture over fish. Drizzle hot oil over all. Garnish with minced green onion and serve at once. Makes 2 servings.

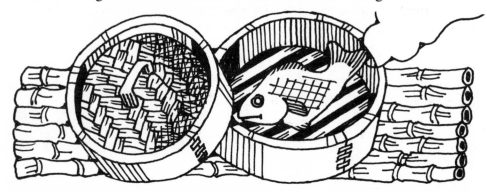

FISH WITH SEASONED DRESSING
layers of delicate, savory stuffing complement your favorite white fish

1 pound fish fillets or steaks (halibut, haddock,
    cod, flounder or any white fish)
1 cup dried bread crumbs
1/4 cup butter or margarine, melted
1/4 cup chopped fresh parsley
1/2 teaspoon dill weed
1 cup shredded zucchini, squeezed free of liquid
1 cup shredded carrots, squeezed free of liquid
1 green onion, minced
1 small green pepper, slivered

Bring fish to room temperature and set aside. In a bowl combine bread crumbs and melted butter, mixing to moisten crumbs. Stir in parsley, dill weed, zucchini, carrots and green onion, mixing thoroughly. In the bottom of a 1 quart heatproof dish that will fit inside steamer, arrange half of the crumb mixture. Arrange fish pieces in an even layer and top with remaining crumb mixture. Steam 15 to 20 minutes, or until fish flakes when tested with a fork. (During last 5 minutes of cooking, arrange pepper slivers over topping and continue steaming.) Serve at once. Accompany with Tartar Sauce, page 40. Makes 6 servings.

QUICK HOMEMADE TARTAR SAUCE

1/2 cup mayonnaise
2 tablespoons pickle relish
1 tablespoon lemon juice
1/4 teaspoon Worcestershire sauce
2 tablespoons finely minced onion

In a small bowl, combine mayonnaise, relish, lemon juice, Worcestershire sauce and onion. Cover and let rest in the refrigerator for at least 1 hour. Makes approximately 3/4 cup. Recipe may be doubled.

COCKTAIL SAUCE

1/2 cup catsup
1 tablespoon lemon juice
1 teaspoon prepared horseradish
1/2 teaspoon Worcestershire sauce
1/8 teaspoon Tabasco sauce

In a small bowl, combine catsup, lemon juice, horseradish, Worcestershire sauce and Tabasco. Cover and chill for at least two hours to allow flavors to blend. Makes 1/2 cup. Recipe may be doubled.

CHEDDAR TUNA MOCK SOUFFLE
make this ahead for a supper that's ready when you are

4 slices bread, cut into cubes
1-1/2 cups shredded cheddar cheese
1 (6-1/2 oz.) can tuna, drained and flaked
1 cup green peas, fresh or frozen and thawed
3 eggs
1 cup milk
1/4 teaspoon pepper
1/2 teaspoon salt

In a greased 1-1/2 quart heatproof dish that will fit inside steamer, layer half of the bread cubes, half of the cheese, all of the tuna, all of the green peas, the remaining bread and remaining cheese. Set aside. In a medium-size bowl, beat together eggs, milk, pepper and salt. Pour egg mixture over bread, cover and let stand at room temperature for 1 hour or up to 24 hours in the refrigerator. Uncover and steam 40 to 50 minutes, or until puffy. Makes 4 servings.

SALMON LOAF
spoon creamy cheese sauce over this before serving

1/2 cup evaporated milk
4 eggs, well beaten
2 tablespoons lemon juice
2 teaspoons dry mustard
1 teaspoon salt
1-1/2 cups soft bread crumbs
1/2 cup minced onion
1 cup diced celery
1/2 cup chopped fresh parsley
1 (16 oz.) can salmon, drained and flaked

In a large bowl, combine milk, eggs and lemon juice with mustard, salt, bread crumbs, onion, celery and parsley. Stir well to moisten dry ingredients. Add flaked salmon and blend thoroughly. In a heatproof dish that will fit inside steamer, mound salmon mixture into a loaf shape. Steam 1 to 1-1/4 hours or until set. Serve with Cheese Sauce (see recipe page 16). Makes 8 servings.

SALMON WITH SOUR CREAM
a wonderfully elegant dish steamed easily in no time

2 salmon steaks, fresh or frozen and thawed
1/2 teaspoon salt
1 cup sour cream
1/2 cup finely chopped onion
1 teaspoon lemon juice
1/2 teaspoon dried tarragon
1/4 cup chopped fresh parsley, for garnish

Arrange salmon in a single layer in a heatproof dish that will fit inside steamer. Salt lightly and set aside. In a small bowl, mix together sour cream, onion, lemon juice and tarragon. Pour sour cream mixture over salmon and steam for 20 minutes, or until fish flakes easily when tested with a fork. Remove and sprinkle with chopped parsley. Serve immediately. Makes 2 servings.

THREE PAN PAELLA
make this colorful masterpiece your specialty

1/4 pound chorizo sausage, crumbled
4 tablespoons olive oil
6 chicken legs
1 small onion, chopped
1 clove garlic, minced
1 cup uncooked long grain rice
1-1/4 cups chicken broth
1/8 teaspoon (or 3 points) saffron
1/2 cup boiling water

1 cup green peas, fresh or frozen and thawed
6 artichoke hearts, halved
1 tomato, chopped *or* 1 (2 oz.) jar pimentos
6 live clams, prepared for steaming (see
    page 34)
6 uncooked large shrimp, shelled and deveined
    or 6 small frozen lobster tails, thawed
1 (6 oz.) can whole pitted olives, drained

In a large skillet, brown chorizo in 2 tablespoons olive oil until crumbly. Remove sausage, drain and keep warm. In the same skillet, brown chicken until tender; remove, drain and keep warm. In the same skillet, sauté onion and garlic until onion is soft but not browned. Drain off excess fat. In a 1 quart heatproof dish that will fit inside steamer, combine onion, garlic, remaining 2 tablespoons oil, rice and chicken broth. Dissolve saffron in boiling water and stir into rice mixture. Steam rice mixture 20 minutes over medium-high heat, stirring once or twice. When rice is nearly done, add peas, artichokes and tomato. In a second steamer tier, place clams and shrimp. Steam rice and shellfish 5 minutes, or until clams are open and shrimp is pink and firm. When done remove rice mixture to paella pan or other large serving dish. Add olives and chorizo and toss to fluff. Arrange cooked shellfish and chicken legs on top and serve at once. Makes 6 servings.

FLAVORS FROM THE ORIENT

CHINESE STYLE STEAMED RICE
a no-scorch method you'll love

1 cup uncooked long grain rice
cold water

In a large bowl or pan, cover rice with cold water and rub rice between your hands to remove starch. When water is milky white, drain and repeat. Drain rice thoroughly and place in a 1 quart heatproof dish that will fit inside steamer. Add 1-1/2 cups water and steam 15 minutes. Stir and continue to steam 5 to 10 more minutes, or until rice is tender and liquid is absorbed. Makes about 3 cups.

PORK DUMPLINGS
these unique, flower-like tidbits are simple to make

1/2 pound lean ground pork
1 tablespoon soy sauce
1 slice fresh ginger root, finely minced
1 teaspoon cornstarch
1 teaspoon dry sherry

1 teaspoon sugar
1/4 teaspoon salt
1 green onion, finely minced
1/2 cup finely diced water chestnuts
24 to 28 round won ton wrappers*

In a medium-size bowl, combine pork, soy sauce, ginger, cornstarch, sherry, sugar, salt, green onion and water chestnuts. Blend thoroughly, using hands if necessary. In the center of each won ton wrapper, place 1 heaping teaspoon meat mixture. Gather up edges, pushing upper half of filling up, to form a cup 1 inch in diameter. Press to flatten bottom so that dumpling stands. Place dumplings in a single layer, on an oiled steamplate or heatproof dish that will fit inside steamer. Steam over medium-low heat 15 to 20 minutes. Serve hot with Dim Sum Sauce (see recipe page 54). Makes 24 to 28 dumplings.

*If only square wrappers are available, cut off corners to make them round.

STEAMED WON TON
nothing equals the flavor of homemade pork and shrimp stuffed won ton

1/2 pound lean ground pork
1/2 pound shrimp, shelled, deveined and finely minced
1 tablespoon cornstarch
2 green onions, finely minced
1 tablespoon soy sauce
1 egg, beaten
1 cup finely chopped spinach
1/2 teaspoon salt
1/2 teaspoon oriental sesame oil (optional)
1 (1 lb.) package won ton wrappers
vegetable oil

In a large bowl, combine pork, shrimp, cornstarch, onions, soy sauce, egg, spinach, salt and sesame oil. Blend thoroughly, using your hands if necessary. In the center of each won ton wrapper, place 1/2 to 1 teaspoon filling. Moisten all 4 corners with water and fold wrapper in half towards you, making a triangle. Press to seal edges; fold center point up even with straight edge. Pick up won ton and fold unjoined corners behind won ton, away from you. Pinch to seal. Continue until all are filled. (Wrappers dry out very quickly. Keep won ton wrappers and filled won ton covered with a damp towel as much as possible.) To steam won ton, lightly oil steamplate or heatproof dish that will fit inside steamer. Arrange won ton in a single layer. Brush won ton lightly with oil. Steam 15 minutes. Add hot to Won Ton Soup recipe (see page 49) or serve as an appetizer with Dim Sum Sauce (see page 54). Makes 80 to 90 won ton.

Note: Won ton filling may be made ahead and stored up to 2 days if well refrigerated. Steamed won ton may be refrigerated up to 2 days before being reheated. Or freeze steamed won ton for up to 4 weeks. Do not store uncooked, filled won ton.

WON TON SOUP
a classic—made simply in minutes!

1-1/2 quarts chicken broth
1 egg
1 cup finely chopped spinach
1 green onion, minced
15 to 20 steamed won ton

In a saucepan, heat chicken broth to boiling. Beat egg well in a small cup. With a fork in one hand, slowly pour egg into broth; with the fork catch the egg in broth and draw into filaments. Add spinach, green onion and won ton. Reheat to boiling and serve at once. Makes 4 to 6 servings.

CHINESE STEAMED PORK BUNS
a favorite of every dim sum aficionado's

4 to 4-1/2 cups all-purpose flour
1 teaspoon salt
3 tablespoons sugar
1 package active dry yeast
1-1/4 cups warm water
2 tablespoons vegetable oil
Barbecued Pork Filling (recipe follows)
16 (2 by 2 inch) squares waxed paper

In a large mixing bowl, combine 4 cups flour with salt, sugar and yeast. Stir in warm water and oil to form a soft dough. Add more flour as needed to make dough manageable. Turn out onto a lightly floured board and knead 10 minutes, or until smooth and elastic. Cover and let rise in a warm place 1 to 1-1/2 hours, or until doubled in bulk. Punch down and divide dough into 16 equal pieces. Roll or stretch each piece into a 4 inch circle and place 1 tablespoon Barbecue Pork Filling in center and gather up edges, twisting gently to seal. Place each bun seam side up on a piece of waxed paper and let rise in a warm place until dough is puffy and no longer springs back when lightly poked, about 30 to 40 minutes. Place buns directly on steamplate or on heatproof plate, allowing 2 inches between each bun for expansion. Bring water to a full boil before placing buns in steamer. Steam 15 to 20 minutes. Serve hot or cold with Dim Sum Sauce (see recipe page 54). Makes 16 buns.

BARBECUED PORK FILLING FOR STEAMED PORK BUNS

3/4 pound Chinese barbecued pork or Pork
   Strips (see recipe page 52), diced
1 slice fresh ginger root, very finely minced
1 green onion, finely minced
1/4 cup diced water chestnuts
1/4 cup diced canned mushrooms, drained
   and liquid reserved

2 tablespoons liquid reserved from mushrooms
1 tablespoon cornstarch
1 tablespoon sugar
1 tablespoon soy sauce
1 tablespoon oriental oyster sauce (or, if not
   available, soy sauce)
1 tablespoon peanut oil

Have pork, ginger, green onion, water chestnuts and mushrooms at hand so that they may be added quickly as needed. In a small bowl, combine 2 tablespoons reserved mushroom liquid and cornstarch, stirring to blend. In another small bowl, dissolve sugar in soy sauce and oyster sauce. In a wok, heat peanut oil until very hot; add pork and ginger, stir-frying quickly for 30 seconds. Add green onion, water chestnuts and mushrooms; continue to stir-fry for 1 minute. Pour soy sauce mixture down sides of wok and stir-fry for 30 seconds. Add cornstarch mixture and stir-fry until mixture thickens. Remove from wok and let filling cool before making buns. (Mixture may be made ahead and refrigerated for up to 2 days; bring to room temperature before filling dough.)

PORK SPARERIBS OR STRIPS

the authentic flavor of Chinatown's barbecued pork—at home!

1 pound pork spareribs, cut into 1-1/2 inch lengths or pork butt, cut into 1 inch wide strips
1 tablespoon hoisin sauce
2 tablespoons catsup
1 tablespoon honey
1 clove garlic, minced
2 teaspoons sherry
2 tablespoons soy sauce

Place pork spareribs or strips in a shallow bowl. In a saucepan over low heat, combine hoisin sauce, catsup, honey, garlic, sherry and soy sauce. Cook for 10 minutes, stirring occasionally. Pour sauce over pork and marinate overnight, basting occasionally. Next day, place pork directly on steamplate or in heatproof serving dish that will fit inside steamer. Steam over medium-low heat for 1 hour, or until thoroughly cooked, basting occasionally with sauce. Makes 4 servings.

CHICKEN IN OYSTER SAUCE AND NUTS
serve over Steamed Rice for a no-fuss one dish meal

2 cups diced uncooked chicken meat (about 1/2 fryer)
1 teaspoon cornstarch
1 tablespoon soy sauce
1 tablespoon dry sherry
1 teaspoon peanut oil
1 cup whole bamboo shoots, chopped
1 (4 oz.) can button mushrooms, drained and liquid reserved
1 tablespoon oriental oyster sauce
1/2 teaspoon sugar
1/4 cup reserved mushroom liquid
1 cup green peas
slivered almonds

In a medium-size bowl, combine chicken, cornstarch, soy sauce, sherry and peanut oil. Allow to rest for 10 to 15 minutes. Stir in bamboo shoots and mushrooms separating chicken pieces as necessary. In a small bowl, combine oyster sauce, sugar and mushroom liquid, stirring to dissolve sugar. Pour sauce over chicken and stir. Place chicken mixture in a 1-quart heatproof dish that will fit inside steamer; steam over medium-low heat for 20 minutes. Stir in peas, breaking up chicken pieces as needed; continue to steam 5 to 10 minutes, or until chicken is tender and pink color is gone from center. Garnish with slivered almonds. Makes 4 servings.

CHINESE HOT CHILE OIL

1/2 cup peanut oil
1 ounce dried red chile peppers

In an uncovered stainless steel saucepan, heat peanut oil until just below boiling. Remove from heat and add chile peppers. Let stand at room temperature for 12 hours. Strain and store oil in a glass jar. Chile oil will last up to 6 months. Makes 1/2 cup.

To make DIM SUM SAUCE combine equal parts Chinese Hot Chile Oil and soy sauce. Serve in individual saucers with hot Steamed Pork Buns, Pork Dumplings or Steamed Won Ton.

BREADS & SWEET TREATS

ZUCCHINI CARROT BREAD
you'll please the brown bag crowd with this

1 egg
1/2 cup vegetable oil
1/2 cup brown sugar
3 tablespoons molasses
1 teaspoon vanilla
1-1/2 cups all-purpose flour
1/2 teaspoon baking soda
1 teaspoon baking powder

1/2 teaspoon nutmeg
1/2 teaspoon cinnamon
1/2 teaspoon allspice
1/2 teaspoon salt
1 cup shredded carrots
1 cup shredded zucchini
1/2 cup walnuts

In a large bowl, mix together egg, oil, brown sugar, molasses and vanilla. Fold in flour, baking soda, baking powder, nutmeg, cinnamon, allspice and salt. Stir in carrots, zucchini and walnuts, stirring only until batter is just blended. Spoon batter into a greased and floured loaf pan that will fit inside steamer*. Steam 40 to 45 minutes, or until a toothpick inserted into the center comes out clean. Makes 1 loaf.

*See Introduction page 10.

STEAMED BROWN BREAD
a hearty textured bread perfect for a winter's supper

1-1/4 cups whole wheat flour
1/4 cup yellow cornmeal
2 tablespoons brown sugar
1/2 teaspoon baking soda
1/2 teaspoon salt
3/4 cup plain yogurt
1 egg, slightly beaten
2 tablespoons vegetable oil
1/2 cup molasses
1/2 cup walnuts
1/2 cup chopped dates

In a large bowl, combine flour, cornmeal, brown sugar, baking soda and salt. Add yogurt, egg, oil and molasses, mixing until smooth. Stir in walnuts and dates until well blended. Pour batter into a greased and floured loaf pan that will fit inside steamer*. Steam 40 to 45 minutes, or until a toothpick inserted into the center comes out clean. Makes 1 loaf.

*See Introduction page 10.

BANANA NUT BRAN MUFFINS
a nutritious treat for breakfast or for snacks

1 cup bran cereal
1/4 cup milk
1-1/4 cups whole wheat flour, stone ground preferred
1-1/2 teaspoons baking soda
1/2 teaspoon salt
1/2 teaspoon vanilla
1 egg, slightly beaten
1/4 cup vegetable oil
1 ripe banana, mashed
1/3 cup honey
1/2 cup plain yogurt
1/2 cup raisins (optional)
1/2 cup chopped nuts

In a large bowl, combine bran with milk; stir to moisten bran and let rest 5 minutes. In a small bowl, combine flour, baking soda and salt. Set aside. To bran add vanilla, egg, oil, banana, honey and yogurt, stirring until blended. Fold in dry ingredients, raisins and nuts, stirring until batter is just blended. Distribute batter evenly among 12 greased muffin tins and steam 25 minutes, or until top springs back when lightly pressed. Makes 12 muffins.

PICKWICK PEACH PIE
so unique with its oatmeal and nut crust

1 cup quick rolled oats
1/4 cup butter, melted
1/2 cup finely chopped nuts
1/4 cup honey

1/4 teaspoon salt
2 teaspoons vanilla
Peach Filling (recipe follows)

In a small bowl, combine oats, butter, nuts, honey, salt and vanilla. Press into the bottom and up the sides of a 1 quart heatproof dish that will fit inside steamer. Pour in Peach Filling and steam 25 to 30 minutes, or until almost set. Serve at once with whipped cream or ice cream, if desired. Makes 6 servings.

Peach Filling

1 (15 oz.) can sliced cling peaches
1/4 cup chopped dried apricots
1 teaspoon lemon juice

2 teaspoons vanilla
1 egg, slightly beaten

Drain peaches thoroughly, reserving syrup, and set aside. In a saucepan, combine syrup and dried apricots. Cover, bring to a boil, turn off heat and let rest 15 minutes. Stir peaches into apricot mixture along with lemon juice, vanilla and egg. Pour into prepared crust.

RICE PUDDING
an old-time favorite with lots of plump, juicy raisins

1 cup uncooked long grain rice
cold water
2 tablespoons butter or margarine
1 teaspoon salt
2 tablespoons brown sugar
1/2 cup homogenized milk

1 (5.33 oz.) can evaporated milk
1 teaspoon vanilla
1 egg
1/2 teaspoon nutmeg
1 cup raisins

In a 1 quart heatproof dish that will fit inside steamer, cover rice with cold water. Rub rice between your hands to wash off starch. Drain off milky water and repeat. Drain rice thoroughly and add butter, 1 cup water and salt. Steam 20 minutes. Meanwhile, in a medium-size bowl, combine brown sugar, homogenized milk, evaporated milk, vanilla, egg and nutmeg. Stir milk mixture into rice and continue to steam, stirring occasionally, for 15 minutes. Add raisins and steam an additional 5 to 10 minutes or until liquid is absorbed and rice is tender. Makes 6 servings.

OLD FASHIONED EGG CUSTARD
stove-top steaming makes this custard a breeze to prepare

2 cups homogenized milk, at room temperature
3 eggs, at room temperature, well beaten
1/4 cup honey
1 teaspoon vanilla
1/2 teaspoon salt
ground nutmeg

In a medium-size bowl, combine milk, eggs, honey, vanilla and salt. Pour or ladle mixture into custard cups or muffin tins. Steam over medium-low heat 10 to 15 minutes, or until set (custard is set when a knife inserted into the center comes out clean.) Sprinkle each serving with ground nutmeg. Makes 6 one-half cup servings.

HELEN'S APPLE TREAT
sweet, spicy apples ready in minutes

4 large tart apples, cored and sliced
1/4 cup raisins or dates, or a combination
1/4 cup finely chopped walnuts
1 teaspoon cinnamon
1/2 teaspoon nutmeg
1/2 teaspoon lemon juice
1/2 cup honey
1/2 cup half and half (light cream), optional

Place apple slices in 1 quart heatproof dish that will fit inside steamer. In a small bowl, combine raisins, walnuts, cinnamon, nutmeg and lemon juice. Top apples with raisin mixture and drizzle with honey. Steam 20 to 30 minutes, or until apples are tender. Serve with cream, if desired. Makes 4 servings.

FRESH PEARS IN AMARETTO
a delightfully different ending for a special meal

4 ripe fresh pears, cored and peeled
8 tablespoons Amaretto liqueur
1 ounce semi-sweet chocolate, shaved into curls or coarsely grated

Place prepared pears upright in a heatproof dish that will fit inside steamer. Spoon 2 tablespoons liqueur over each pear. Steam 5 minutes and baste with liqueur. Steam an additional 5 minutes or until tender. Remove to individual serving dishes and spoon liqueur over each. Garnish with chocolate curls and serve at once. Makes 4 servings.

STEAMED BANANAS ROYALE
an impressive dessert made with ingredients you have on hand

4 firm ripe bananas
1/2 cup butter or margarine
1/2 cup firmly packed brown sugar
1/2 teaspoon nutmeg
1/2 teaspoon cinnamon
whipped cream, for garnish

Peel and halve bananas crosswise and then in half lengthwise. Place in a heatproof dish that will fit inside steamer. Dot with butter and sprinkle with brown sugar, nutmeg and cinnamon. Steam 3 minutes and baste with melted butter and brown sugar. Steam another 3 minutes and baste again. Steam an additional 4 minutes, or until bananas are tender and brown sugar sauce is combined. Place in individual serving dishes, spooning sauce over all and dollop generously with whipped cream. Serve at once. Makes 4 servings.

RECIPE INDEX